For the Teacher

This reproducible study guide to use in conjunction with the book *The Absolutely True Diary of a Part-Time Indian* consists of lessons for guided reading. Written in chapter-by-chapter format, the guide contains a synopsis, pre-reading activities, vocabulary and comprehension exercises, as well as extension activities to be used as follow-up to the novel.

In a homogeneous classroom, whole class instruction with one title is appropriate. In a heterogeneous classroom, reading groups should be formed: each group works on a different novel at its reading level. Depending upon the length of time devoted to reading in the classroom, each novel, with its guide and accompanying lessons, may be completed in three to six weeks.

Begin using NOVEL-TIES for reading development by distributing the novel and a folder to each student. Distribute duplicated pages of the study guide for students to place in their folders. After examining the cover and glancing through the book, students can participate in several pre-reading activities. Vocabulary questions should be considered prior to reading a chapter; all other work should be done after the chapter has been read. Comprehension questions can be answered orally or in writing. The classroom teacher should determine the amount of work to be assigned, always keeping in mind that readers must be nurtured and that the ultimate goal is encouraging student's love of reading.

The benefits of using NOVEL-TIES are numerous. Students read good literature in the original, rather than in abridged or edited form. The good reading habits formed by practice in focusing on interpretive comprehension and literary techniques will be transferred to the books students read independently. Passive readers become active, avid readers.

Novel-Ties® are printed on recycled paper.

SYNOPSIS

Arnold ("Junior") Spirit is growing up on the Spokane Reservation in Washington State. The reservation is an inhospitable place for a gifted boy who was born with water on the brain and some resulting medical problems. Arnold's greatest consolation is pen and paper, with which he creates brilliant cartoons that express his view of his world. Life on the "rez" is not all bleak for Junior: he loves his parents, flawed as they are, looks up to his eccentric sister Mary, and adores his grandmother. He has a pugnacious best friend, Rowdy, who has stuck by him through the many crises of childhood. For better or worse, he belongs to a tribe.

But when a teacher counsels Junior to transfer from Wellpinit High to Reardan, a school off the reservation, loyalties shift and old assumptions give way to new questions. Rowdy turns against Junior, leaving him without the ballast of their friendship and making him wonder each day if he has lost something more precious than what he has gained by entering mainstream culture.

Once enrolled at Reardan High, Junior must prove his worthiness to his new teachers, the students — and most of all, to himself. In order to fit in, he pretends to be middle class, hiding his poverty and insecurities from Penelope, a sometime girlfriend, and Roger and Gordy, new friends whose loyalties have yet to be tested. Amazingly, Junior manages to carve out a niche for himself at Reardan High that he never managed to create at Wellpinit, succeeding academically and on the basketball court. Life seems to be improving, despite Junior's ambivalence and a nagging sense that he is at once a part-time Indian and a part-time white person.

These issues are crystallized by a series of shocking deaths that tear the fabric of Junior's life. As he loses his beloved grandmother, a close family friend, and then his sister, Junior despairs of finding happiness as a tribal Indian. What the Spokane culture offers in beauty and tradition, it has lost in grinding poverty and alcoholism, two contributors to early and violent death. Junior simultaneously loves and loathes what the reservation symbolizes.

The intense basketball games between Reardan and Wellpinit pit Indian against white, bringing into the physical realm all the ambivalence in Junior's psyche. Winning and losing become freighted with more meaning than even a tournament game should hold, as Junior finds out when the affluent Reardan team ultimately defeats the impoverished Spokane players.

In the midst of his grief for all those he has lost, Junior manages to regain his friendship with his childhood friend. He will not give up what he has found in Reardan, but neither will he turn his back on the reservation. If only for a moment, the two young men are able to play together without keeping score.

BACKGROUND INFORMATION

The Tribes and the Reservation System

The Indian Removal Act of 1830 allowed the U.S. government to legally relocate tribes to circumscribed areas known as reservations. These were almost always created on lands that were remote and inferior for hunting and agricultural purposes. Eastern tribes were forced to relocate west of the Mississippi River; western tribes were made to give up large areas of their traditional lands, disrupting long-established patterns and creating poverty and want. Separated geographically and culturally from the emerging European society, Indians had little to gain and almost everything to lose from their transactions with the newcomers.

It soon became obvious that Indian societies were in crisis. The federal government intervened with the Dawes Act (1887), intended to replace communal ways with the institution of private property. It was thought that by dividing lands into small farms and ranches, tribal people would become economically self-sufficient and would begin to think like Europeans. The failure of the Dawes Act to reestablish the well-being of Indians led the government to support new policies. From the mid-twentieth century on, emphasis was placed on mainstreaming Indians into modern society through various social services, such as educational and employment programs. Today, it is estimated that no more than twenty-five percent of Indians live on reservations.

Those who do remain on the reservations have not fared well. With the exception of the casino businesses established by some tribes, job opportunities are extremely limited, schools are poor, and poverty is the inevitable result. The high rates of alcoholism and premature death that characterize reservation life are signs that the crisis in Indian culture continues. The Bureau of Indian Affairs, created in 1842 and still functioning today, has so far failed to find adequate systems for interrupting the cycle of poverty. Today, Indians represent the most impoverished of all America's minority groups. Over a third of all American Indians live below the poverty line, whether on or off the reservation.

The Spokane

The Spokane Indians of Washington State are an ancient tribe whose language classifies them as a Salish people, linguistically related to tribes in British Columbia, Idaho, and Montana. The traditional subsistence of the Spokane depended upon hunting, gathering, and fishing the salmon of the Spokane River. Like many tribes, the Spokane moved camp according to the seasons, following fishing and harvesting patterns centuries old. Gradual changes to the tribal culture came about from exposure to the Plains Indians, from whom they discovered the many uses of the horse, and from cultural contact with other native peoples.

The greatest change for the Spokane resulted from contact with whites. These early relationships were usually benign, as white traders were often assimilated into the tribe through friendships and intermarriage. Later contacts, however, were catastrophic: the Gold Rush of 1849 and the white migration West brought Indians and whites into vio-

lent conflict. With their native lands exploited and food sources threatened, the Spokane, like many other tribes, found their traditional way of life imperiled. Damming the Columbia River, in particular, was disastrous for the Spokane, who have long depended upon the supply of salmon.

While there were whites who were concerned for the welfare of the tribes, it seemed that simple humanity and compassion were no match for the relentless thrust of settlers into the old Indian territories. The Spokane were forced to move to reservations and began their long legal battle with the U.S. government to get compensation for their reduced livelihood in the fishing industry.

About the Author

Poet and storyteller Sherman Alexie was born in 1966 on the Spokane Indian Reservation into the Spokane/Coeur d'Alene tribe. The award-winning author, like his protagonist in *The Absolutely True Diary of a Part-Time Indian*, faced physical and social challenges in his early childhood that caused him great suffering and later alienated him from his peers.

Other important details of the author's youth form the basis of this autobiographical novel for young adults. Alexie transferred from the reservation school at Wellpinit, attended Reardan High, and became a star basketball player. Later, he attended Gonzaga University and Washington State University, where he originally took pre-med courses. He did not go on to medical school, having discovered a love of poetry.

Alexie is an extremely versatile writer. In addition to the many volumes of poetry and fiction, he has authored songs and a screenplay. Many of his literary works explore the relationship between Indian and white culture. Alexie is also known as a compelling public speaker and stand-up comedian. He and his family live in Seattle, Washington.

PRE-READING ACTIVITIES AND DISCUSSION QUESTIONS

1. Preview the book by reading the title and the author's name and by looking at the illustration on the cover. What do you think the book will be about? What do you think might be the central conflict in the story? Thumb through the book, looking at the illustrations. What do these pictures reveal about the book and about its author/illustrator?

2. Read the Background Information on page three of this study guide and do some additional research to learn more about the reservation and its effect on tribal people. Find out about government acts and policies, tribal leadership, and problems in Indian society today. Record information in the first two columns of a K-W-L chart, such as the one below. Fill out column three after you finish the book.

What I Know −K−	What I Want to Learn −W−	What I Learned −L−

3. In this novel, the main character must come to terms with his identity as both an Indian and as an individual. What other works of fiction have you read in which cultural identity plays a significant role in the character's central conflict?

4. The novel focuses on several characters who are gifted in some way. How might the possession of a special talent or ability enrich someone's life? On the other hand, how might it cause problems in someone's life?

5. The author of this novel uses many of his own experiences to create the character of Junior Spirit. Like his protagonist, the author had to overcome physical and emotional challenges as well as a cultural conflict. What do you suppose happens when a person has many obstacles, such as these, to overcome? Do you think that facing challenges makes a person stronger?

6. A stereotype is an oversimplified image of a group of people, usually held in common by some part of society. How can stereotypes be harmful? What do you think people can do to overcome stereotyping? Have you noticed any examples of stereotyping in your community or in the media? Are there stereotypes of American Indians that affect how you think about them?

7. Grief is an emotion that all human beings experience at some point in their lives. With a group of classmates, discuss how grief might affect us and why the process of grieving is unlike any other emotional journey.

8. The game of basketball is an important element of this novel. How does being a member of a team develop a person's character? What kinds of interpersonal skills are required to be a good team player?

The Black-Eye-of-the-Month Club; Why Chicken Means So Much To Me; Revenge is My Middle Name; Because Geometry is Not a Country Somewhere Near France

Vocabulary: Draw a line from each word on the left to its definition on the right. Then use the numbered words to fill in the blanks in the sentences below.

1. susceptible
2. impediments
3. smirked
4. hypothermia
5. vandalism
6. inseparable
7. minions
8. decrepit

a. favorites or followers
b. intentional damage to property
c. easily affected or influenced
d. broken down
e. obstacles or physical defects
f. smiled in a silly or self-satisfied manner
g. life-threatening cold body temperature
h. that which cannot be parted

. . . .

1. After repeated acts of _____ were committed on our house, we decided to move out of the neighborhood.

2. The queen entered the great hall, surrounded by her _____.

3. The _____ state of the old house suggested that it had been abandoned many years earlier.

4. Although the twins were _____ as children, they now led independent lives.

5. Very young and very elderly people are the most _____ to infection.

6. I was insulted when you _____ at my attempt to sing.

7. Visitors to the arctic regions must beware of _____.

8. Stuttering and lisping are two common speech _____.

> Read to find out about life on the Spokane Reservation.

Questions:

1. Why did Junior consider himself abnormal? What factors reinforced this self-image?

2. How was the prejudice of the white dentist revealed?

3. Why didn't Junior blame his father for shooting Oscar?

The Black-Eye-of-the-Month Club; Why Chicken Means So Much To Me; Revenge is My Middle Name; Because Geometry is Not a Country Somewhere Near France (cont.)

4. What factors contributed to the bond between Junior and Rowdy? What part did comic books play in Rowdy's life?

5. What does the cartoon on page six show about Junior's deepest desires? What was the role of art in his life?

6. Why was Junior shocked at finding his mother's name on his math textbook?

Questions for Discussion:

1. Why do you think alcoholism is widespread on Indian reservations?

2. Why do you suppose that Junior's sister Mary "froze" after high school? What does the picture of her suggest about her way of coping with life?

3. How do you think Junior would be treated by his peers at your school? Would you want to be his friend?

4. Why do you imagine Junior described the reservation as "approximately one million miles north of Important and two billion miles west of Happy"?

5. Why do you suppose geometry appealed to Junior? How might mathematical certainties contrast with the rest of his experiences?

Literary Devices:

I. *Hook*—A hook refers to an opening passage in a work of fiction that is sufficiently intriguing to propel the reader into the book. What is the hook at the beginning of this book?

_____

_____

II. *Metaphor*—A metaphor is a suggested or implied comparison between two unlike objects. For example:

> . . . my mother and father are the twin suns around which I orbit and my world will EXPLODE without them.

What is being compared?

_____

How does the comparison suggest the nature of Junior's relationship with his parents?

_____

_____

The Black-Eye-of-the-Month Club; Why Chicken Means So Much To Me; Revenge is My Middle Name; Because Geometry is Not a Country Somewhere Near France (cont.)

III. *Point of View*—Point of view refers to the voice telling the story. It could be one of the characters or the author narrating. From whose point of view is the story told?

_____

Why do you think the author chose this point of view?

_____

_____

Social Studies Connection:

Do some research to learn more about the history and current status of the Spokane tribe. How is the Spokane reservation governed? What work is available on or near the reservation? How do Spokane officials and the U.S. government agencies work together? Prepare a brief oral report.

Art Connection:

Draw a comic strip based on an incident in this section of the novel. Choose an event that is not already illustrated. Add captions to your comic strip to explain the action.

Writing Activity:

Write a journal entry that explores how you see yourself in contrast to how others might see you. You may choose to add illustrations to your pages.

Hope Against Hope; Go Means Go; Rowdy Sings the Blues; How to Fight Monsters; Grandmother Gives Me Some Advice

Vocabulary: Synonyms are words with similar meanings. Draw a line from each word in column A to its synonym in column B. Then use the words in column A to fill in the blanks in the sentences below.

A	B
1. contemplating	a. prejudiced
2. literally	b. threatening
3. depressed	c. considering
4. defeated	d. clear
5. mutilated	e. conquered
6. translucent	f. actually
7. racist	g. butchered
8. impending	h. saddened

. . . .

1. We rowed back to shore quickly as the _____ storm darkened the sky.

2. Everyone expects our basketball team to be _____ by the older, stronger, and better trained team we are playing against.

3. After studying dinosaurs, our class is _____ a trip to the natural history museum.

4. Our beautiful garden was _____ when crowds of walkers used it as a shortcut to the stadium across the street.

5. After the rain, _____ droplets of water made the leaves shimmer.

6. Certain that I had never shown behavior that could be seen as prejudiced, I was insulted when you called me a(n) _____.

7. When the weatherman said you could fry an egg on the sidewalk in the heat, he didn't mean it _____.

8. The man was so _____ that he decided to see a therapist.

> Read to find out how Junior makes a life-changing decision.

Hope Against Hope; Go Means Go; Rowdy Sings the Blues; How to Fight Monsters; Grandmother Gives Me Some Advice (cont.)

Questions:

1. How did Junior break Mr. P's nose? What were the consequences of this action?

2. What did Mr. P mean when he told Junior that teachers had intended to "kill the Indian to save the child"? Why did Mr. P apologize to Junior?

3. How did Mr. P change Junior's view of his sister Mary?

4. Why did Mr. P insist that Junior go to school off the reservation?

5. Why did Junior call Hope "a mythical creature"?

6. Why did Rowdy suddenly turn against Junior? How did his reaction fulfill Mr. P's prediction?

7. How did the prejudice Junior encountered in Reardan differ from the prejudice he had experienced in Wellpinit?

8. How did Junior's confusion over the unwritten rules of behavior at Wellpinit lead to the incident with Roger?

Questions for Discussion:

1. Do you think that Mr. P was justified in telling that "You're going to find more and more hope the farther and farther you walk away from this sad, sad, sad reservation"?

2. Were you surprised that Junior decided to transfer to the Reardan school?

3. Do you think Junior's grandmother was right when she assessed Roger's behavior? If not, why do you think Roger didn't challenge Junior to a fight or seek revenge?

4. Should Junior now expect to be accepted by the boys at Reardan? What will he need to do to fit in?

Literary Elements:

I. *Setting*—Setting refers to the time and place of events in a work of literature. What are the two main settings of *The Absolutely True Story of a Part-Time Indian*? How does each setting help to shape the action of the story?

_____

_____

Hope Against Hope; Go Means Go; Rowdy Sings the Blues; How to Fight Monsters; Grandmother Gives Me Some Advice (cont.)

II. *Conflict*—A conflict in literature is a struggle between opposing forces. There are three kinds of conflicts:

- person *vs.* person
- person *vs.* nature
- person *vs.* self (inner struggle)

In the chart below, record those conflicts that you found so far in this book. When you finish reading the novel, think about whether each conflict was resolved.

CONFLICT

Type of Conflict	Details
person *vs.* person	
person *vs.* nature	
person *vs.* self	

Science/Nature Connection:

Research "pack order" in dog and wolf populations. How do these animals in groups show dominance, submission, and form other social relationships? Organize your findings as a poster, comic strip, or other graphic. Post your art on the classroom bulletin board. Discuss with your classmates how these examples of behavior in animals can also be found in human behavior.

Writing Activity:

Rowdy becomes Junior's enemy when he learns that his friend plans to transfer to a white school. Write about a time when you or someone you know had a friendship abruptly end because of an action taken. What were the circumstances? If the situation occurred again, do you think you would act in the same way?

Tears of a Clown; Halloween; Slouching Toward Thanksgiving; My Sister Sends Me an Email; Thanksgiving; Hunger Pains

Vocabulary: Read each group of words. Cross out the one word that does not belong with the others. On the line below the words, tell how the remaining words are alike.

1. innocent   inexperienced   naive   sophisticated

    The other words are alike because _____

2. assaulted   attacked   encountered   struck

    The other words are alike because _____

3. sensitive   vulnerable   exposed   guarded

    The other words are alike because _____

4. drive   force   depth   momentum

    The other words are alike because _____

5. aggressive   pathetic   pitiful   wretched

    The other words are alike because _____

6. boring   curious   tedious   monotonous

    The other words are alike because _____

> Read to find out whether Junior fits in at Reardan.

Questions:

1. According to Junior, why did he always have a problem getting girls to like him?
2. Why did Junior want to collect money for the homeless on Halloween?
3. Why didn't Mr. Dodge accept Junior's explanation of the process that creates petrified wood?
4. Why was Junior lonelier at Reardan than he had ever been before?
5. Why were Junior's parents disappointed in their daughter Mary's marriage?
6. Why was Gordy a suitable friend for Junior? What did Junior learn from him?
7. According to Mary's letter, what were the main differences between the Spokane Reservation and the Flathead Reservation?
8. Why did Junior think it was odd that his family celebrated a typical American Thanksgiving?
9. What formed the initial bond between Junior and Penelope?

Tears of a Clown; Halloween; Slouching Toward Thanksgiving; My Sister Sends Me an Email; Thanksgiving; Hunger Pains (cont.)

Questions for Discussion:

1. Which do you think is worse—being physically attacked by your peers or being ignored?

2. In what ways do you think Mary's elopement inspired Junior to acts of courage?

3. How would you compare the relationship between Junior and Penelope to a typical teenage romance? What role did ego and insecurity play in the relationship?

Literary Devices:

I. *Irony*—Irony is a literary technique that involves a twist of fate or presents an outcome that is opposite of what is expected. Why was it ironic that Junior collected money for the homeless? Why was it ironic that Penelope collected money, too?

_____

_____

II. *Flashback*—A writer can play with time sequence to achieve particular effects. A flashback is a scene that takes the narrative back to a time before the current point in the plot. What do you learn about Junior's emotions from the flashback at the beginning of the chapter, "Tears of a Clown"?

_____

_____

III. *Simile*—A simile is a figure of speech in which two unlike objects are compared using the words "like" or "as." For example:

> PCs are like French people living during the bubonic plague.

What is being compared?

_____

_____

What does this reveal about Gordy's way of thinking and expressing himself?

_____

_____

Tears of a Clown; Halloween; Slouching Toward Thanksgiving; My Sister Sends Me an Email; Thanksgiving; Hunger Pains (cont.)

Literary Element: Characterization

Use the Venn diagram below to compare Junior with his two new friends—Gordy and Penelope. Record the traits they have in common in the overlapping parts of the diagram.

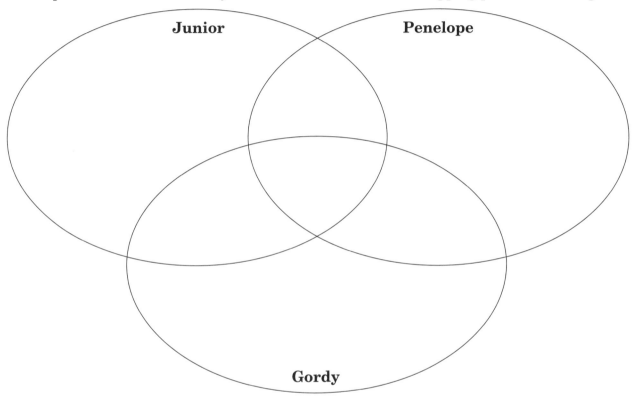

Health Connection:

Do some research to find out about the causes and effects of the eating disorders anorexia and bulimia. How do the symptoms of these disorders vary? What types of treatment are available today? How serious are these disorders? Present your findings in an oral report.

Writing Activity:

Sometimes, people who seem confident on the surface have underlying worries and insecurities. Write about a time when you discovered that someone you liked and admired had secret fears or issues.

Rowdy Gives Me Advice About Love; Dance, Dance, Dance; Don't Trust Your Computer; My Sister Sends Me a Letter; Reindeer Games; And A Partridge in a Pear Tree

Vocabulary: Use the context to help you determine the meaning of the underlined word in each of the following sentences. Then draw a line from each numbered word below to its definition on the right.

- The puppy ran around in circles, <u>ecstatic</u> at all the attention the children paid him.

- Fearing that tourists would consider them <u>primitive</u>, the local Indians traded their tribal costumes for jeans and tee-shirts.

- I spoke out against my government even though I knew it would cause me to be <u>banished</u> from my country.

- <u>Predators</u> such as lions and tigers are said to be high on the food chain.

- Tables holding cups of water were lined up along the route of the <u>marathon</u>.

- Being a shy person, I find that large parties tend to <u>intimidate</u> me.

- Winners in a competition should show good sportsmanship, never expressing <u>contempt</u> for the losers.

. . . .

1. ecstatic	a.	forced to leave; dismissed
2. primitive	b.	animals that prey on other animals
3. banished	c.	to make fearful
4. predators	d.	overwhelmed with joy
5. marathon	e.	disrespect; scorn
6. intimidate	f.	uncivilized
7. contempt	g.	long-distance race

> Read to find out what happens when Junior confesses to poverty.

Questions:

1. Why did Junior conclude that "Gordy the bookworm was just as tough as Rowdy"?

2. Why was Junior ashamed of being poor? How did this pretense affect his life?

3. How was Junior's life changed when he revealed his poverty?

4. How did Gordy help Junior understand why Rowdy and others on the reservation considered him a traitor?

Rowdy Gives Me Advice About Love; Dance, Dance, Dance; Don't Trust Your Computer; My Sister Sends Me a Letter; Reindeer Games; And A Partridge in a Pear Tree (cont.)

5. Why did Junior's father tell him about the way he met Junior's mother?

6. Why was Junior chosen for the varsity basketball team?

7. What did the basketball game at Wellpinit reveal about the attitude of the Spokane toward whites? Why did the people from the reservation jeer at and taunt Junior?

8. What action showed that Junior's father felt guilty for his behavior at Christmas?

Questions for Discussion:

1. How much do you think Junior's attraction to Penelope was based on racial and cultural differences?

2. Why do you think Junior saw being Indian as a "part-time job"?

3. Do you agree with Junior's conclusion that "if you let people into your life a little bit, they can be pretty damn amazing"?

4. Do you think Junior's parents were sufficiently supportive of their son? Could they have done more to help him?

5. Vince Lombardi, coach for the Green Bay Packers, is quoted as saying, "The quality of a man's life is in direct proportion to his commitment to excellence, regardless of his chosen field of endeavor." What do you think Lombardi meant? Do you agree?

Cooperative Learning Activity:

Work with a group of your classmates to predict what will happen in the novel. In the chart below, record your predictions in response to each of the following questions.

Question	Prediction
1. What role might Coach play in Junior's life?	
2. How will Junior's self-esteem be affected by playing varsity basketball?	
3. Will Junior's relationship with Penelope develop further?	
4. Will Rowdy and Junior become friends again?	
5. Will Junior ever come to terms with being a part-time Indian?	

Rowdy Gives Me Advice About Love; Dance, Dance, Dance; Don't Trust Your Computer; My Sister Sends Me a Letter; Reindeer Games; And A Partridge in a Pear Tree (cont.)

Social Studies Connection:

Do some research to find out about the casino business on Indian tribal lands. How did this business get started? What have been the economic and social effects on various tribes? Prepare notes for a discussion group to be held with some classmates.

Writing Activities:

1. Imagine that you are a sports reporter covering the Reardan-Wellpinit game. Describe what occurred and discuss why the events unfolded as they did.

2. Imagine that you were in the hospital room and write a brief dialogue that could have taken place between Junior and Coach.

Red Versus White; Wake; Valentine Heart; In Like a Lion

Vocabulary: Antonyms are words with opposite meanings. Draw a line from each word in column A to its antonym in column B. Then use the words in column A to fill in the blanks in the sentences below.

	A		B
1.	eccentric	a.	precisely
2.	tolerant	b.	casual
3.	intact	c.	planned
4.	vaguely	d.	encourage
5.	formal	e.	dull
6.	spontaneous	f.	broken
7.	scintillating	g.	common
8.	demoralize	h.	biased

. . . .

1. In the morning, I _____ recalled the odd dream of the previous night.

2. The jeers and insults of the other team were meant to_____ our players.

3. The panel of famous journalists held a(n) _____ discussion about recent world events.

4. With his odd mannerisms and way of speaking, Sherlock Holmes may be considered a(n) _____ character.

5. In writing a business letter, it is proper to adopt a(n) _____ tone.

6. I tripped while carrying the cake box, but luckily the strawberry shortcake remained _____.

7. People think my sister's jokes are scripted, but they are actually _____.

8. Because he was known as a(n) _____ person, everyone was shocked when the coach would not let one of his players observe his religious holiday.

> Read to find out how a basketball game becomes the defining moment in Junior's life.

Questions:

1. Why did Junior begin to appreciate his parents more after attending school in Reardan?

2. According to Junior, what was his grandmother's best quality? Why did he value this quality so highly?

3. Why was Junior accepted back into tribal society?

Red Versus White; Wake; Valentine Heart; In Like a Lion (cont.)

4. Why did so many people attend Grandmother's funeral?
5. Why did the mourners at the funeral laugh?
6. What did Mrs. Spirit's refusal of the tribal costume reveal about her?
7. How did Eugene's death underscore the hopelessness and despair of reservation life? What was Junior's reaction to this second tragedy?
8. Why did Junior compare himself to Medea in one of the plays of Euripides, a fifth century BC Greek writer?
9. What sparked the protest of Junior's classmates? Why did Junior find their protest absurd?
10. How did Coach demonstrate confidence in Junior's playing?
11. What turned the Reardan win into a sour experience for Junior?

Questions for Discussion:

1. Why do you suppose that Indians were traditionally more accepting of individual differences than whites? Do you think there are exceptions to this generalization?
2. What do you think motivates people like Billionaire Ted to attach themselves to Indian culture? Do you agree with Junior that this interest in Indian culture by whites should always be criticized?
3. How do you suppose the activity of list-making helped Junior heal from grief?
4. When Junior reached the end of his rope and could not sustain the agony he felt, he turned to cartooning as a way to search for answers and be able to face life. Do you think this is a good thing to do? What do you do?
5. Do you think Junior exaggerated the negative role that alcohol plays on Indian reservations? What do you think might help solve the problem? Why hasn't the problem been solved?
6. Do you agree with Junior in the power of expectations—that if you are expected to do well, you are more likely to succeed? And conversely, if no one expects anything of you, you are more likely to fail?

Social Studies Connection:

Do some research to learn about the tradition of the powwow. What purposes have these tribal ceremonies served? How has the custom varied from one Indian tribe to another? Prepare an oral report to present to a group of classmates.

Writing Activities:

1. Write a journal entry about a loss you have experienced. Whom or what did you lose? How did this experience affect you?
2. Write about a victory that was bittersweet for you. What factors made you enjoy your victory? What factors made the experience somewhat sour?

Rowdy and I Have a Long and Serious Discussion About Basketball; Because Russian Guys are Not Always Geniuses; My Final Freshman Year Report Card; Remembering; Talking About Turtles

Vocabulary: Word analogies are equations in which the first pair of words has the same relationship as the second pair of words. For example: NARROW is to WIDE as NEAR is to DISTANT. Both pairs of words are opposites. Choose a word from the Word Box to complete each of the analogies below.

WORD BOX			
arrogance	destiny	plummeting	summit
chronic	dormant	sibling	

1. FATE is to _____ as VALUE is to WORTH.

2. FATHER is to PARENT as SISTER is to _____.

3. HUMILITY is to _____ as GENEROSITY is to GREED.

4. FEARFUL is to SCARED as CONSTANT is to _____.

5. _____ is to HIBERNATION as WILTED is to DECAY.

6. ASCENDING is to _____ as LABORING is to RESTING.

7. _____ is to MOUNTAIN as FLOOR is to OCEAN.

Read to find out whether Junior and Rowdy resume their friendship.

Questions:

1. What did the email exchange between Rowdy and Junior suggest about their relationship?

2. How did Mary's death confirm Junior's darkest fears about his identity?

3. Why did Rowdy blame Junior for Mary's death? How did Junior react to Rowdy's charge against him?

4. How did listing the tribes to which he belonged help Junior redefine himself?

5. How was Rowdy finally able to forgive Junior for leaving the reservation and going to Reardan?

Rowdy and I Have a Long and Serious Discussion About Basketball; Because Russian Guys are Not Always Geniuses; My Final Freshman Year Report Card; Remembering; Talking About Turtles (cont.)

Questions for Discussion:

1. Why do you think Junior laughed uncontrollably upon learning of Mary's death? How do you explain this emotional reaction?

2. Why do you think Junior had attended so many Indian funerals? What does the comparison of white and Indian death rates suggest?

3. Why do you think Junior was comforted more by his return to school than by the presence of his extended family at the wake?

4. Do you think it is possible to love and to hate something at the same time? In what ways does Junior simultaneously love and hate the reservation?

5. Why do you think Rowdy would not accept Junior's challenge to join him at Reardan the following year?

6. From what you know about Junior and Rowdy, do you think they could be friends as adults? Would they be enemies?

Literary Device: Flashback

What is the narrative purpose of the lengthy flashback in the chapter "Talking About Turtles"?

Literary Element: Characterization

In the chart below show the ways that Junior and Rowdy changed from the beginning of the book to the end. Which one changed the most?

	Beginning of Novel	**End of Novel**
Junior		
Rowdy		

Rowdy and I Have a Long and Serious Discussion About Basketball; Because Russian Guys are Not Always Geniuses; My Final Freshman Year Report Card; Remembering; Talking About Turtles (cont.)

Science Connection:

Do some research to find out how a lake can catch fire. What unusual circumstances can cause this to happen? What examples can you find of burning lakes? Prepare a poster that shows natural processes that can make lakes catch fire.

Writing Activity:

Write about a time when you were able to forgive someone. What were the circumstances? What helped you to let go of your anger?

CLOZE ACTIVITY

The following passage has been taken from the chapter "Dance, Dance, Dance." Read it through completely. Then fill in each blank with a word that makes sense. Afterwards, you may compare your language with that of the author.

Traveling between Reardan and Wellpinit, between the little white town and the reservation, I always felt like a stranger.

I was half Indian in one place _____ [1] half white in the other.

It was _____ [2] being Indian was my job, but it _____ [3] only a part-time job. And it _____ [4] pay well at all.

The only person _____ [5] made me feel great all the time _____ [6] Penelope.

Well, I shouldn't say that.

I _____, [7] my mother and father were working hard _____ [8] me, too. They were constantly scraping together _____ [9] money to pay for gas, to get _____ [10] lunch money, to buy me a new _____ [11] of jeans and a few new shirts.

_____ [12] parents gave me just enough money so _____ [13] I could pretend to have more money _____ [14] I did.

I lied about how poor _____ [15] was.

Everybody in Reardan assumed we Spokanes _____ [16] lots of money because we had a _____. [17] But that casino, mismanaged and too far _____ [18] from major highways, was a money-losing _____. [19] In order to make money from the _____, [20] you had to work at the casino.

_____ [21] white people everywhere have always believed that _____ [22] government just gives money to Indians.

And _____ [23] the kids and parents at Reardan thought _____ [24] had a lot of money, I did _____ [25] to change their minds. I figured it _____ [26] do me any good if they knew _____ [27] was dirt poor.

What would they think _____ [28] me if they knew I sometimes had _____ [29] hitchhike to school?

Yeah, so I pretended _____ [30] have a little money. I pretended to _____ [31] middle class. I pretended I belonged.

Nobody knew the truth.

POST-READING ACTIVITIES

1. Return to the K-W-L chart on tribal people that you began in the Pre-Reading Activities on page four of this study guide. Add or change any information in column one and fill in column three. Compare your responses with others who have read the same book.

2. Return to the conflict chart that you began on page ten of this study guide. Add new information and enhance the information that you have already presented. Compare your responses with those of others who have read the same book.

3. Return to the predictions chart that you began on page fifteen of this study guide. Which of these predictions turned out to be accurate? Which do you need to revise?

4. Now that you have finished reading the book, why do you think the author chose *The Absolutely True Diary of a Part-Time Indian* for the title? What other title might be appropriate for this autobiographical novel?

5. **Pair/Share:** In this book, many of the characters face serious obstacles, but they respond very differently to their circumstances. With a partner, discuss the problems that these characters confront and analyze how each reacts to circumstances. Who are the "survivors" in this story? What do they have in common?

6. Based on the novel, do you think the author felt more hopeful or saddened by the experience of young people who remain on the reservation? Explain your answer.

7. **Art Connection:** What role do you think the sketches and cartoons play in this novel? How would this book have been different without these illustrations? Choose an event from the book that was not illustrated and provide a cartoon that would go along with it. Then choose an event from your own life, describe it in text and draw a cartoon to illustrate it.

8. **Art Connection:** Junior creates numerous sketches and cartoons that depict people in his life and his own emotional states. Using photographs, sketches, cartoons, paintings or other materials, create a collage that shows who or what is important in your life. Consider displaying your artwork in the classroom.

9. **Drama Connection:** Select a memorable chapter from *The Absolutely True Diary of a Part-Time Indian* and write a dramatic scene based on the events. With one or more classmates, rehearse this scene, adding your own dialogue if you wish. Perform your scene for the whole class.

10. *The Absolutely True Diary of a Part-Time Indian* is based loosely on the youth of author Sherman Alexie. Write a short story based on some significant issue or event in your life. Share your story with a group of classmates.

Post-Reading Activities (cont.)

11. **Literary Element: Theme**—A theme in a literary work is its controlling idea or message. *The Absolutely True Diary of a Part-Time Indian* has several important themes. Consider the following themes and discuss how each is developed in the novel:

    - individual identity *versus* conformity to social expectations
    - coming to terms with loss
    - overcoming stereotypes
    - concern with self *versus* concern for others
    - the power of art and literature
    - the human need for self-expression
    - forming ties with others

12. **Literature Circle:** Have a literature circle discussion in which you tell your personal reactions to *The Absolutely True Diary of a Part-Time Indian*. Here are some questions to help your literature circle begin a discussion.

    - Do you identify with Junior in any way? Why? Do you identify with any other character?
    - Did this book provide you with any new insights into the lives of people you would never have known otherwise?
    - Do you think the characters and the way they spoke were presented in a realistic fashion? Why or why not?
    - Which character did you admire the most? The least?
    - Who else would you like to read this novel? Why?
    - If you could have a discussion with Sherman Alexie, the author of this book, what would you ask him?

SUGGESTIONS FOR FURTHER READING

Fiction

Bruchac, Joseph. *The Journal of Jesse Smoke: A Cherokee Boy, The Trail of Tears, 1838*. Scholastic.

Cannon, A.E. *The Shadow Brothers*. Random House.

Childress, Alice. *A Hero Ain't Nothin' But a Sandwich*. HarperCollins.

* Cisneros, Sandra. *The House on Mango Street*. Random House.

Dorris, Michael. *A Yellow Raft in Blue Water*. Warner Books.

_____. *Morning Girl*. Hyperion.

Doyle, Roddy. *Paddy Clarke Ha Ha Ha*. Penguin.

Erdoes, Richard, and Alfonso Ortiz, eds. *American Indian Myths and Legends*. Random House.

Erdich, Louise. *The Birchbark House*. Scholastic.

Gregory, Dick. *Nigger*. Simon & Schuster.

Joyce, James. *Portrait of the Artist as a Young Man*. Penguin.

* Kingsolver, Barbara. *The Bean Trees*. HarperCollins.

_____. *Pigs in Heaven*. HarperCollins.

* Mohr, Nicholas. *El Bronx Remembered*. HarperCollins.

Monture, Joel. *Cloudwalker: Contemporary Native American Stories*. Fulcrum.

Nonfiction

* Angelou, Maya. *I Know Why the Caged Bird Sings*. Random House.

Brown, Dee. *Bury My Heart at Wounded Knee*. Simon & Schuster.

DeLoria, Vine Jr. *Custer Died for Your Sins: An Indian Manifesto*. Simon & Schuster.

Mihesuah, A. Devon. *American Indians: Stereotypes and Realities*. Clarity Press.

Riley, Patricia, ed. *Growing Up Native American: An Anthology*. HarperCollins.

Some Other Books by Sherman Alexie

The Lone Ranger and Tonto Fistfight in Heaven. Grove/Atlantic Monthly.

One-Stick Song. Hanging Loose Press.

Toughest Indian in the World. Atlantic Monthly Press.

Smoke Signals: A Screenplay. Hyperion.

The Man Who Loves Salmon. Limberlost Press.

The Summer of Black Widows. Hanging Loose Press.

Indian Killer. Atlantic Monthly Press.

Water Flowing Home. Limberlost Press.

Reservation Blues. Atlantic Monthly Press.

* NOVEL-TIES Study Guides are available for these titles.

ANSWER KEY

The Black-Eye-of-the-Month Club; Why Chicken Means So Much to Me; Revenge is My Middle Name; Because Geometry is Not a Country Somewhere Near France

Vocabulary: 1. c 2. e 3. f 4. g 5. b 6. h 7. a 8. d; 1. vandalism 2. minions 3. decrepit 4. inseparable 5. susceptible 6. smirked 7. hypothermia 8. impediments

Questions: 1. Junior considered himself abnormal because he was born with extra fluid on the brain (hydrocephaly) and because in the aftermath of surgery, he was mildly disabled. The taunting of his peers reinforced his negative self-image. 2. The prejudice of the white dentist was revealed in his assumption that Indians experienced less physical pain than whites. 3. Junior didn't blame his father for shooting Oscar because he accepted his mother's honest explanation about the veterinary expenses involved in treating the dog, comprehending as he did that the family was trapped in a cycle of poverty. 4. The bond between Junior and Rowdy was based on a shared birthday, a common sense of being misfits in reservation society, and an attraction to comic books. These books provided escapist fantasy for Rowdy, an alternative to his depressing life. 5. The cartoon on page six shows that Junior is desperate to carve out a niche for himself through imagination and creativity. Art served to ease his loneliness, express deep feelings, and was also a plea for acceptance and understanding. 6. Junior was shocked at finding his mother's name on his math textbook because this made him realize the textbooks had not been replaced or updated in thirty years, a fact which underscores the inadequacy of the reservation school system.

Hope Against Hope; Go Means Go; Rowdy Sings the Blues; How to Fight Monsters; Grandmother Gives Me Some Advice

Vocabulary: 1. c 2. f 3. h 4. e 5. g 6. d 7. a 8. b; 1. impending 2. defeated 3. contemplating 4. mutilated 5. translucent 6. racist 7. literally 8. depressed

Questions: 1. Junior broke Mr. P's nose accidentally when he hurled his math book across the room in a fit of anger; as a consequence, Junior was suspended from school and suffered from feelings of guilt. 2. When he told Junior that teachers had intended to "kill the Indian to save the child," Mr. P was referring to the attempt to forcibly mainstream Indian students into white culture. Mr. P apologized to Junior because he was trying to make amends to him and to all the other students to whom he had acted inhumanely. Now he wanted to help bright youngsters reach their potential. 3. Mr. P changed Junior's view of his sister Mary, someone he saw as being tough and unsentimental, to someone who was sensitive and had dreams of being a writer. 4. Mr. P insisted that Junior go to school off the reservation in order to experience a more hopeful atmosphere and realize his academic potential. 5. Junior called Hope "a mythical creature" because he had rarely if ever met a person who actually felt hopeful. 6. Rowdy suddenly turned against Junior because he felt betrayed and left behind by Junior's decision to transfer; he felt he could not make it off the reservation himself, and wanted to hold Junior back, too. Mr. P had predicted that Rowdy would become increasingly mean and eventually turn against Junior. 7. The prejudice Junior encountered in Reardan was racial, while the prejudice he had experienced in Wellpinit was related to his disability and perceived "differences." 8. Junior's confusion over the unwritten rules of behavior at Wellpinit led to the incident with Roger because Junior had been conditioned to fight physically when insulted and did not realize that a fight could take place on a purely verbal level.

Tears of a Clown; Halloween; Slouching Toward Thanksgiving; My Sister Sends Me an Email; Thanksgiving; Hunger Pains

Vocabulary: 1. sophisticated–the other words are alike because they describe a lack of experience of the world. 2. encountered–the other words are alike because they describe an act of aggression. 3. guarded–the other words are alike because they describe the condition of being defenseless. 4. depth–the other words are alike because they describe thrust or forward motion. 5. aggressive–the other words are alike because they describe a state of unhappiness or misery. 6. curious–the other words are alike because they describe something that is lacking in interest value

Questions: 1. Junior believed his problems with girls were caused by his preference for girls who were out of his league, and thus unattainable. 2. Junior wanted to collect money and pool it with Penelope's collection in order to make a romantic connection with her, rather than for the altruistic reason she presumed. 3. Mr. Dodge didn't accept Junior's explanation of the process that creates petrified wood because the teacher was a racist who assumed that a poor Indian student would not understand scientific principles, and because he himself had little knowledge of the subject. 4. Junior was lonely at Reardan because he was ignored by all his peers and his teachers had no respect for his intelligence. 5. Junior's parents were disappointed that their daughter married an Indian from another reservation in Montana that had different customs and traditions, and that

she would be traveling with her poker-playing husband far from home. 6. Gordy was a suitable friend for Junior because he, like Junior, was intelligent, curious, and original; Gordy taught Junior to nurture his intellect, appreciate the world around him, value his cartooning skill, and become comfortable with his originality. 7. According to Mary's letter, the main differences between the Spokane Reservation and the Flathead Reservation were the comparative affluence of the Montana environment and the partial integration of the reservation, with whites and Indians residing on the same site. 8. Junior thought it was odd that his family celebrated a traditional Thanksgiving because the Pilgrims and their descendants had tried to obliterate the Indian population. 9. Junior's advice "not to give up" on herself and a desire by Penelope to transcend the ordinary and rebel against her father's norms formed the initial bond between the two.

Rowdy Gives Me Advice About Love; Dance, Dance, Dance; Don't Trust Your Computer; My Sister Sends Me a Letter; Reindeer Games; And a Partridge in a Pear Tree

Vocabulary: 1. d 2. f 3. a 4. b 5. g 6. c 7. e

Questions: 1. Junior concluded that Gordy was as tough as Rowdy when they both responded in a similar way to Junior's request for advice about his relationship with Penelope. They both accused Junior of buying into the stereotype about white women and thus displaying racist attitudes. 2. Junior was ashamed of being poor because he thought people equated poverty with worthlessness. He thought that if others knew that he had no money, it would reflect negatively upon him, his family, and his tribe. 3. When Junior disclosed the truth about his financial situation, it lifted a heavy burden from him as he could finally accept the sympathy and help of friends. 4. Gordy explained to Junior that communities evolved when people banded together for survival and protection. Conformity and a shared mission was necessary, but individualism and nonconformity were seen as a threat. According to Gordy, this is why some on the reservation thought Junior was a traitor. 5. Junior's father told him the story about meeting Junior's mother in order to encourage Junior to imagine possibilities where there seemed to be none. In this case, he subtly encouraged Junior to try out for the basketball team. 6. The qualities that earned Junior a place on the varsity team were persistence, courage, and heart, in addition to his skill as a shooter. 7. The basketball game at Wellpinit revealed that the attitude of Indians toward whites was one of hostility and resentment. The people of the reservation jeered at Junior because he had become a symbol to the tribe of all that they distrusted and hated in oppressive white society. 8. Saving the five-dollar-bill for Junior showed that his father felt guilty for getting drunk and staying away at Christmas.

Red Versus White; Wake; Valentine Heart; In Like a Lion

Vocabulary: 1. g 2. h 3. f 4. a 5. b 6. c 7. e 8. d; 1. vaguely 2. demoralize 3. scintillating 4. eccentric 5. formal 6. intact 7. spontaneous 8. tolerant

Questions: 1. Junior began to appreciate his parents more after attending school in Reardan because he compared them to more affluent whites who ignored their children and saw that his mother and father cared about him and made sacrifices for him, despite their troubles. 2. According to Junior, his grandmother's best quality was tolerance; he valued this quality because he had seen that ugliness stemmed from lack of it. Her tolerance even extended to the drunk driver who caused her death. 3. Junior was accepted back into reservation society because the loss of his Grandmother transcended his so-called betrayal of the code of the tribe. 4. So many people attended Grandmother's funeral because she had traveled around to different reservations and gained the respect and friendship of many people. 5. The mourners at the funeral laughed because Billionaire Ted had made a fool of himself by attempting to return a valuable costume to the wrong tribe. 6. Mrs. Spirit's refusal of the costume revealed that she had absolute integrity and would not accept the costume on false pretenses although it would have brought in money. 7. Eugene's death underscored the despair and hopelessness of reservation life in which chronic alcoholism among the population led to pointless deaths. Junior's reaction to this second tragedy was one of contempt both for the ravages wrought by alcohol and the insufficient consolation of religion. He responded by turning to books and by using his cartooning as catharsis. 8. Junior compared himself to Medea who asked "What greater grief than the loss of one's own native land?" He identified with this grief as part of the Indian nation that had lost so much that even murder could be understood. 9. Mrs. Jeremy's insensitive treatment of Junior sparked the protest of his classmates. Junior found it absurd that they had walked out without him, as if he were a symbol rather than a person. 10. Coach demonstrated confidence in Junior's playing by assigning him the job of guarding Rowdy, Wellpinit's star player. 11. The realization that Reardan had defeated the underdog, the poor Spokanes, turned the Reardan win into a sour experience for Junior. He wanted to apologize for beating a team that had overcome amazing odds to play as they had all year. He had mixed feelings of allegiance and guilt for wanting to exact a measure of revenge.

Rowdy and I Have a Long and Serious Discussion About Basketball; Because Russian Guys Are Not Always Geniuses; My Final Freshman Year Report Card; Remembering; Talking About Turtles

Vocabulary: 1. destiny   2. sibling   3. arrogance   4. chronic   5. dormant   6. plummeting   7. summit

Questions: 1. The email exchange between Rowdy and Junior suggested that their relationship was no longer hostile and might return to its earlier warmth. 2. Mary's death confirmed Junior's darkest fears about his identity by suggesting that the fate of an Indian is to lose everything of value and to die young. 3. Rowdy blamed Junior for Mary's death because Junior had set an example in leaving the reservation school. Junior reacted to this accusation by accepting the blame and feeling responsible. 4. By listing the tribes to which he belonged, Junior redefined himself as a unique individual and as a human being as well as a Spokane. It also made him realize that he might always be lonely and an outsider in any one of his worlds, but that he would survive and have a better life than if he remained on the reservation. 5. Rowdy was finally able to forgive Junior for transferring out of Wellpinit's school by comparing Junior to the nomads who spent their lives searching for the sources of survival. Although he now approved of this nomadic life, Rowdy knew he would remain on the reservation.